THE ANIMAL WALL

THE ANIMAL WALL

and other poems

GILLIAN CLARKE

illustrated by Karen Pearce

PONT *poetry*

First Impression—1999

ISBN 1 85902 654 0

This book is published with the support of the
Arts Council of Wales.

Printed in Wales at
Gomer Press, Llandysul, Ceredigion

for
Cai, Coyan, Llaima Mali, Jake, Ifan, Elis, Cai & Manon.

Special thanks are due to Angharad and Betsan for reading and listening to the poems. I am also grateful to Matthew Williams, Curator at Cardiff Castle, for his help.

Acknowledgements are due to the following publications where some of these poems, or versions of them, first appeared: *Collected Poems,* Carcanet; *Five Fields,* Carcanet; *Alchemica,* Oriel Mostyn; *The Whispering Room,* Kingfisher; *Prickly Poems* and *Paws and Claws,* Hutchinson*; Dear Future, A Time Capsule of Poems,* Hodder; *The Times Educational Supplement*; *The New Exeter Book of Riddles,* edited by Lawrence Sail and Kevin Crossley-Holland. Thanks are also due to the following for commissioning and giving some of these poems their first performance*:* Equilibre; Theatr Powys; Central Television for *'In the Barn'*.

CONTENTS

WHAT SANDRA SAID   9

THE ANIMAL WALL   10

NAIN CHOOSES A HAT   18

THE BOX-KITE   20

ANNIE   21

THE VET   22

STEALING PEAS   23

THE PADDLE-STEAMERS   24

BREAKING THE HORSE   25

BALANCING   26

HORSE OF THE SEA   28

THE SHIRE HORSE   29

THE MAN IN THE WILDERNESS   30

IN THE BARN   32

IN THE TIME OF THE WOLF   33

NEWT   34

THE OSPREY   35

THE DREAM-CATCHER   36

JAC THE CAT   37

CHIP-HOG   38

SPRING RIDDLE   40

SUMMER RIDDLE 41

THE SWORD FROM AFRICA 42

MY BOX 43

THE LAKE GIRL'S SONG 44

THE TITANIC 45

BRANWEN'S SONGS 46

BREAKING STONES 48

THE VILLAGE SHOP 49

THE HONEY MAN 50

STORM 51

SUMMER-WATER SONNET 52

THE HAND-GLASS 53

LETTERS FROM BOSNIA 54

IF I LIVED 55

WINTER RIDDLE 56

OLD CAT 57

A VERY COLD LAMB 58

A POEM A DAY 59

NOTES 60

WHAT SANDRA SAID

'You know how lovely it is
when you're sitting by the window,
in a big chair,
and it's raining,
and you have a book,
and you think:
How lucky I am!
How lucky!'

THE ANIMAL WALL

Two lions, a lynx,
a lioness,
a bear, a seal,
a pair of apes,
wolf, hyena,
vulture, beaver,
leopard, racoons,
anteater, pelican
under the moon.

*

Street Boy crouches in the dark
under the wall in the Castle park.
New Year's Eve. It begins to snow.
Street Boy doesn't know where to go.

His mother's left, his Dad is cruel.
He hardly ever goes to school.
He stinks. He filches things. He spits.
He can't read and he's got nits.

His father's taken to the drink.
Sister in care, brother in klink.
He's hungry, thirsty, cold and sad
with his Mam gone and his Dad gone mad.

*

10

He quietly creeps
into the street
as the sixtieth second
of the sixtieth minute
of the twenty fourth hour
of the very last day of the year
melts with a shiver
like snow in the river,
and the midnight hour
strikes from the tower.
All the bells begin to ring.
Something is about to begin.

*

More than a hundred years ago
a rich man saw the castle grow.

Masons, carpenters, carvers and gilders,
scaffolders, painters, artists and builders.

They sculpted stone with chisel and hammer
in dusty workshops, winter and summer.

As he watched them grow, how the rich man loved
the way the animals slowly shoved

and shouldered out of the stone to loll
lazily on his Castle wall.

*

The city'll be awake all night,
streets awash with noise and light.
Street Boy's out late,
dawdling past the Castle gate
towards the bridge over the river.
He touches each beast to feel it quiver,
counts them all
on the Castle wall.

Lions, lynx,
lioness,
a bear, a seal,
a pair of apes,
wolf, hyena,
vulture, beaver,
leopard, racoons,
anteater, pelican
under the moon.

*

As he calls them by their names
stone cold hearts and stone cold brains
warm up, wake up, begin to beat
under the clock in Castle street

He strokes each one
in its coat of stone.
Their eyes of glass
saw the century pass.

A yawn. A purr. The animals stir.
Lovely Lions, Lioness,
a pride of big cats
prowls the darkness.

Slinky Lynx wakes up and yawns,
stretches its body newly born.
Golden limbs slip from the stone
to hunt in the hours before dawn.

Sliding from the wall, the Bear
puffs out a breath of silver air,
scoops from the river a shoal of stars,
and catches the moon in his powerful paws.

Slither-beast, fin-foot,
slippery Seal,
morlo, sea-calf,
born from the sea.

Two loving Apes,
picking fleas,
hugging each other's
hairy knees.

Wild Wolf howling
at the moon.
Grey Wolf singing
his mournful tune.

Hyena laughter
echoes alone.
Aardwolf after
blood and bone.

Vulture, bin-thief, carrion-eater,
tip-scavenger, street-sweeper,
wind-soarer, make-away,
robber of delis and take-aways.

Beaver builds his bivouac
from a pile of logs and a rubbish sack.
He takes the river in his stride
and bridges it from side to side.

Lapidary Leopard leaps
on silent paws into the street.
Along the frozen road it goes
leaving roses in the snow.

Racoons in the tinsel light of the street.
Revellers pass on dancing feet.
They waver along as daft as balloons,
too drunk to notice two little racoons.

Anteater entertains a young
ant colony, uncoils his tongue
like a party popper with a pantomime feather,
and swallows a mouthful of bitter weather.

Pelican plucks
breast-feather-flakes
till pavement and street
are white with the work
of her rucksack beak
and her elegant feet.

*

They sniff and lick Street Boy's cold feet
and then lope off down Westgate Street.
Through rowdy crowds their shadows go
like childhood dreams in the falling snow.

Together they warm their paws and hands
in the breath of an extractor fan
from the kitchen of a posh hotel,
and raid the bins outside the *Angel*.

They growl and purr,
they rip and tear.
They guts and guzzle
till they're full to the muzzle
with turkey, stuffing,
gravy and pudding.
They swallow and slurp
and gulp and burp,
with slops and leavings,
scraps and scrapings,
crusts and peel,
grateful for a stolen meal.

Together they leap without a sound
the wall of the new rugby ground,
prowl the stadium for a lark,
and roar like the ghosts of the old Arms Park.

Up Golate to St Mary Street,
on silent feet
Street Boy and animals go
chasing their shadows
in the falling snow,
tonight, tomorrow,
and long ago.

A streak of light in the eastern sky.
A sleek police car cruises by.
The party's over. Taxis creep
from the city to where the suburbs sleep.
A gritter-lorry spits out salt.
Lights go on in a block of flats.
A bus lights up and leaves the station
sweeping shadows into motion.
A milk-float whines along and stops
with a chink of bottles on every step.

*

One by one the beasts slink home.
Street Boy walks in the dawn alone
through burst balloons and party streamers,
lager cans and homeless dreamers.

He walks with Lions,
Lioness, Lynx,
Bear and Seal,
the pair of Apes,
Wolf, Hyena,
Vulture, Beaver,
Leopard, Racoons,
Anteater and Pelican
who one by one
turn to shadows
then to stone.

NAIN CHOOSES A HAT

Seventeen hats,
and the sun pours into the city.
Outside the window, across the street
the Saturday park is green and gold.

Seventeen hats
in felt, straw, linen. A peacock trails
his emerald, indigo, violet ribbons
on the Castle walls.

Seventeen hats
on a long mahogany counter.
The assistant is patient. My mother
fixes me with a hat-pin stare.

Seventeen hats,
and the golden afternoon growls
where stone wolf, lioness, leopard and lynx
bask in the sun on the castle wall.

Hats like mushrooms, row upon row.
Saturday's leaking away.
I'm ten, and I'm taller than her.
I breathe on the big store window.

She's trying on feathers, flowers, fruit.
She's fingering ribbons of satin and silk.
She likes navy, beige, dove grey, black.
She's not sure they suit.

She tries on the peacock on the castle wall.
She tries a stone lion. She tries on a lynx.
She tries on a wolf. It eats her
and the hats. It eats them all.

They forgot there's a wolf inside
every child caged in a city store
while Nain on a visit spends golden hours
Saturday shopping for hats.

THE BOX-KITE

I wanted it, dreamed of it, saved for it,
went to town with my father to buy it.
We spread the scaffolding
and its silky geometry
filled with air and light.

Yellow parachute silk,
the King of kites.
We took it to the rec
and gave it to the wind.
It flew far and small as a comet.

Then lightness turned fierce,
the string with its delicate purr
became live wire in my hands
as if at the deep-end of the sky
a great fish thrashed in the currents.

The wind stole it from me,
my gold sky-box.
Ever since, whenever
a gale blows in my heart,
I lose it again.

ANNIE

(1868-1944)

I called her Ga, and a child's stuttered
syllable became her name.
A widow nearly forty years,
beautiful and straight-backed,
always with a bit of lace about her,
pearls the colour of her coiled hair,
the scent of lavender.

> It was our job at Fforest to feed the hens
> with cool and liquid handfuls of thrown corn.
> We looked for eggs smuggled in hedge and hay,
> and walked together the narrow path to the sea
> calling the seals by their secret names.

At Christmas she rustled packages under the bed
where the 'po' was kept and dusty suitcases.
That year I got an old doll with a china face,
ink-dark eyes and joints at elbows and knees.
Inside her skull, like a tea-pot, under her hair,
beneath her fontanel, was the cold cave
where her eye-wires rocked her to sleep.

> Somewhere in a high hospital window –
> I drive past it sometimes with a start of loss –
> her pale face made an oval in the glass
> over a blue dressing-gown. She waved to me,
> too far away to be certain it was her.
> They wouldn't let children in.
> Then she was lost or somebody gave her away.

21

THE VET

'Would the child like to leave?
It won't be pleasant.'
But I'm stuck with it,
brazening out the cowshed
and the chance of horror,
not knowing how to leave
once I'd said I'd stay.

Gloved to the elbow in blood
and her mysterious collar of muscle,
he wrenched from the deep cathedral of her belly
where her heart hung and the calf swam in its pool,
a long bellowing howl
and a rope of water.

I got off lightly that time,
no knife, no severing,
no inter-uterine butchery
to cut them free.

He let go the rope of water
and the calf swam home like a salmon
furled in a waterfall,
gleaming, silver, sweet under the tongue
of his brimming mother.

STEALING PEAS

Tamp of a clean ball on stretched gut.
Warm evening voices over clipped privet.
Cut grass. Salt fish from the mudflats,
and the tide far out.

He wore a blue shirt
with an *Aertex* logo,
filthy with syrups of laurel and rhododendron,
the grime of a town park.

We crawled in the pea rows
in a stolen green light,
pea-curls catching the tendrils of my hair,
peas tight in their pods as sucklers.

We slit the skins with bitten nails,
and slid the peas down the chutes of our tongues.
The little ones were sweet,
the big ones dusty and bitter.

'Who d'you like best?'
Beyond the freckled light of the allotment,
the strawberry beds, the pigeon cotes,
a lawn-mower murmured and the parky shouted
at a child we could not see.

'You're prettier. She's funnier.'
I wish I hadn't asked.

THE PADDLE-STEAMERS

Dawn a quiver on a bedroom ceiling,
and it's quick, up and away,
with bread, cheese, windfalls
and a bottle of dandelion burdock,
the flash of clean white daps on the pedals.

Drop your bike on the stones.
Step under the echoing cold of the pier.
Pick lapis-blue mussels and amberweed necklaces
from the terrible stanchions of rust.
Wait for the paddle-steamer rounding the headland.

Sometimes it's me in the prow
of *Glen Usk, Ravenswood, The Cardiff Queen,*
waves oiling apart to port and starboard,
light a slither of water-snakes,
a whiplash of metals and mermaid hair.

The tide goes out, taking its time.
Away it slides over the mud-flats
leaving a gleam of pebbles, crustacea, driftwood,
and a rusty bicycle without wheels.

BREAKING THE HORSE

She listens
ear to the ground
for the beat that might be
her own heart.

The horse comes
flickering,
muscular as water,
like a man
but without his thunder.

She lies quiet
in the grass.
It comes sidelong.
It shares her breath,
the moss of its muzzle.

She bridles it with glances,
slow as water
lapping its body,
hoof, fetlock, shoulder,
its beautiful head.

She numbers the vertebrae
as the sea counts the stones,
lays her head
on the thundering ribcage,
kneels till he takes
the bitten apple.

BALANCING

for a Lippizana mare called Capriole

'A question of balance', he said,
leaning the small weight of his body
against the air. Beneath the press of his thigh
the mare stepped away, hoof over delicate hoof,
catching his weight again.

She did it perfectly, as if
concentrating, or listening
to a beat deeper than music,
tacking the seas of her brain
under gravity's shifting centre.

And somewhere in horse-memory
out there under the moon
a stallion danced hoof over hoof
before the sleepy mares,
his blood on fire.

Stamping starlight from wet grass,
he turned the planet under his hooves,
as the moon inched west,
drawing the sea's veined silver
like a horse's skin.

HORSE OF THE SEA

Great water horse
whose steps are moonlight,
whose bridle is the wind,
whose mane is the wild sea,
whose whinny is the creak
of the rigging.

Black horse of ocean
whose spittle is spindrift,
whose sinews are currents,
whose skin is water,
whose bones are ships' spars,
whose heart is the drumming wave.

Horse of the sea,
seven riders on his back,
and one holding on to his tail,
brought Elidir to Gwynedd
from the lands of the Old North,
Scotland to Wales.

Du'r Moroedd.
See him tow the long salt ropes
over the sound, deeps and shallows,
and rise from the sea in a dazzle of light
on a beach in Anglesey,
to claim a Kingdom.

THE SHIRE HORSE

Who knew the land better than this Shire?
She and her kind into the weather leaning,

a horse, a man, an acre of land to plough
in a day, her patient power churning

stubborn earth to a tilth that's fit for seed.
Man and horse and quiet acre turning

to face the dusk, a scattered chaff of stars,
and a cold spring dream of barley, the field singing

as a hand of wind passes, shadows slide
over the tall corn, the ripe seed ringing.

The loft will brim with grain. Below
he'll hear her stamp in her stall, breathing

scents of the hay she carried. Her gift
is strength, but the century's eroding

her tracks from a land where in her hoof-prints, harvest,
and every harvest since came springing.

THE MAN IN THE WILDERNESS

The man in the wilderness said to me,
'How many strawberries grow in the sea?'
I answered him as I thought good,
'As many as herrings grow in the wood.'

The man in the wilderness said to me,
'How many stars in the sky?' said he.
I stare at the moon till it makes me shiver
And I wonder and wonder, who made Forever?

The man in the wilderness said to me,
'Who's that breathing in the sycamore tree?
Who goes by on a silver hoof,
Rattling windows, tapping the roof?

When you're lying in bed at night,
What's that thing like slithery light
That slides through the curtains and down the wall,
Under the door and into the hall,

Like a flat star falling out of the sky,
Whenever a car goes driving by?
What's that ticking in the central heating?
Whose heart's that so loudly beating?'

The man in the wilderness said to me,
'How many buckets would empty the sea?'
Who-who's that crying in the cold night air?
Who-who? Who-who? Who-who goes there?'

How many strawberries? How many stars?
Herrings, owl-cries, passing cars?
How many galaxies, more or less?
Oh! get lost, man in the wilderness!

IN THE BARN

In the old oak beam
is the rustling forest

In the fork of the roof
is the pigeon's nest

In the mound of hay
is the summer meadow

In the web-winged bat
is the flittering shadow

In the fox and the owl
are the night-bringers

In the gaps between stones
are the wind's fingers

In the glittering frost
are the cold stars

In the cracks in the roof
are silver bars

In the puddle on the floor
is the moon's face

In the thawing stream
is spring's voice

In the creak of the door
is the swallow's cry

In the hole in the shutter
is the sun's eye

IN THE TIME OF THE WOLF

Who sings the legend?
  The mouse in the rafters,
  the owl in the forest,
  the wind in the mountains,
  the tumbling river.

Where can we read it?
  In a shadow on the grass,
  in the footprint in the sand,
  in reflections on the water,
  in the fossil in the stone.

How shall we keep it?
  In the lake of history,
  in the box called memory,
  in the voice of the teller,
  in the ear of the child.

How will we tell it?
  With a tongue of lightning,
  with a drum of thunder,
  with a strumming of grasses,
  with a whisper of wind.

NEWT

Secretive amphibian
in the night garden,
she lurks in her stone den,
or hunkers under the coal
so you'll never tell
where her nest is hidden.

But in summer
search the pond at night
by torchlight
for the little moon-bright
dinosaur
in her lair.

Little dragon
of the garden,
asleep at noon,
she's up late stitching a cot
to a leaf of water-crowfoot.
by the light of the moon.

THE OSPREY

Suddenly from the sea,
a migrating angel on its way
from Lapland to Africa
took a break at Cwmtydu.
It stayed three weeks,
like the moon roosting in an oak.

They fed it like a pet
on slithering buckets of silver
left over from the fish shop.
You could tell it was happy
by the way it splintered the sun
with its snowbird wings.

But its mind was on Africa,
the glittering oceans, the latitudes
sliding beneath its heart.
'Stay!' they said. 'Stay!'
But one day it lifted off and turned south
for the red desert, for the red sun.

THE DREAM-CATCHER

I made a nest of maidenhair,
an old sea-rope and whitened bones,
the broken ribs of telephones
and salt-bleached branches all stripped bare.

I made a nest of coloured string
and hung it in the stinking air
where wind and tide were everywhere
and water made the flute-bones sing.

I filled my nest with sand and foam,
a drowned lamb's wool, a dolphin skull,
the lamentation of a gull,
a dogfish egg, a mermaid's comb.

At low tide in the heat of noon
I made my nest of bladderwrack.
But night flew home in crackling black
and left the warm egg of the moon.

JAC THE CAT

Jac the cat's
gone wild,
got the wind
on his mind.
Can't sleep,
can't lie,
green fire
in his eye.
On the branch
of the stair
quivering Jac
in his lair.
Cobweb shivers
in the air.
Wind's shoulder
at the door.
At the window
lion's claw.
In the chimney
something breathes.

Sheet of paper
on the floor
stirs the dust
with a white paw.
Jac trembles,
Jac flies.
Got the sun
in his eyes,
got the wind
on his mind.
I can't stand
another minute.
Out! Storm!
And Jac with it!

CHIP-HOG

Hog-of-the-road,
leaf-scuffer,
little tramp of the lanes –

like the old bearded one
wheel-wobbling his bicycle,
weighed to the saddle
with string bags, ropes,
a rosary of tin mugs,
or hunkered down for the winter
under threadbare thatch.

Pin-cushion,
boot-brush,
flea-bag,
eye-in-the-leaf-pile.

One fifth of November
we lifted him just in time,
safe on a shovel from the smoke
of his smouldering house,
his spines sparking like stars.

Milk-scrounger,
slug-scavenger,
haunter of back doors and bins.

Once, kissing goodnight at the gate,
we saw a ghost:
something white,
something small,
something scratching,
headlong, hell-bent, heel-over-tip hedgehog,
head in a chip-bag and hooked
on his own prickles,
the last chip escaping him
as fast as he could run.

SPRING RIDDLE

Suddenly, on a silent gardening day,
two notes from half a mile away.

Did we hear it? Too far, too deep
in trees stirring their bones from sleep

to be quite sure. Again. A voice.
C and A flat. Treacherous sweetness

in two clear notes across the valley's well
of silence and the winds of April.

We set our tools aside and listen hard
to hear it calling from the leafless wood,

excited once more by a summer guest
who pitches camp inside a plundered nest,

grows fat on murder, and in a stolen house
rehearses two notes in an angel's voice.

SUMMER RIDDLE

All afternoon I hope
it'll come back – rope

of sunlight, silence,
something silk, a sibilance,

the turning pages of a book,
a breath that made me look.

It parts the grass
just long enough to pass.

A word unspooled from somewhere,
the fluent freehand signature

of flood, of cool *couleuvre*
in a most un-Roman swerve

of Celtic knotwork, the heart's
blood-beat, the holy art

of gilding in the grass, a glance
of flame, of flamboyance.

THE SWORD FROM AFRICA

He brought back a sword
wrapped in cloth of gold.

She brought hunger,
animals on the dusty road,
skeletons of cattle, horses, goats,
wreckage of bones in the burning sun.

She brought wandering tribes
in their frayed embroideries,
the glittering gaze
of beautiful, starved faces.

She brought torn robes and broken saddles,
beaded silks and camel rugs,
treasures from the broken kings
of the desert.

She brought the shrivelled grasp
of a baby's hand,
its body a dry husk
in her arms.

She brought the sun
in its cloth of gold,
the bloody, burning
sword of war.

MY BOX

My box is made of golden oak,
my lover's gift to me.
He fitted hinges and a lock
of brass and a bright key.
He made it out of winter nights,
sanded and oiled and planed,
engraved inside the heavy lid
in brass, a golden tree.

In my box are twelve black books
where I have written down
how we have sanded, oiled and planed,
planted a garden, built a wall,
seen jays and goldcrests, rare red kites,
found the wild heartsease, drilled a well,
harvested apples and words and days
and planted a golden tree.

On an open shelf I keep my box.
Its key is in the lock.
I leave it there for you to read,
or them, when we are dead,
how everything is slowly made,
how slowly things made me,
a tree, a lover, words, a box,
books and a golden tree.

THE LAKE-GIRL'S SONG

I'm the lake-king's daughter
and my element is water,
but earth and air are joy
and I love the farmer's boy.

So I'll leave my blue sky ceiling
for a roof of slate.
I'll leave my cold green room,
my water-weed curtains,
my bed of water-crowfoot,
my blanketweed,

for a cool white attic
with a window of sky,
a white lace curtain
and a deep feather-bed,
pillows of goose-down
and a Welsh wool quilt.

The farmer's boy will love me,
the sun shine above me.
I'm the lake-king's daughter
from the cold grey water.

THE TITANIC

Under the ocean where water falls
over the decks and tilted walls
where the sea comes knocking at the great ship's door,
the band still plays
to the drum of the waves,
to the drum of the waves.

Down in the indigo depths of the sea
the white shark waltzes gracefully
down the water-stairway, across the ballroom floor
where the cold shoals flow,
and ghost dancers go,
ghost dancers go.

Their dresses are frayed, their shoes are lost,
their jewels and beads and bones are tossed
into the sand, all turned to stone,
as they sing in the sea
eternally,
eternally.

Currents comb their long loose hair,
dancers sway forever where
the bright fish nibble their glittering bones,
till they fall asleep
in the shivering deep,
in the shivering deep.

BRANWEN'S SONGS

When the King of Ireland
tired of me,
they took my child,
my velvet and my gold,
my place at table,
my peace, my grace,
my bed of goosedown,
my maid,
my husband,
my heavy crown.
They gave me the scullery,
the servants' cruelty,
a stone floor,
a bed of straw.

*

Day after day
a starling came to my hand,
both of us small birds at a window.
He, with a dark rainbow in every feather,
took seed and crumbs from me,
touched my hand like rainfall.
I told him my name,
until he held its two syllables
of water in his throat,
two pearls to bear across the sea
on a prevailing westerly.

I threw him into the wind
calling, 'Branwen! Branwen!'
to the far horizon.

*

When my eloquent starling left my hand
I grieved alone, and for a month or more
my eyes never left the grey and empty sea.

Then when the wind cried all night on the land,
huge waves breaking on the troubled shore,
I woke to hear my child cry in my dream.

At dawn swineherds ran breathless to the King
with tales of an island, trees, two lakes, all
moving shoreward on the morning swell.

There, through the waves, my brave Brân striding,
his tall fleet dancing at his heel
like giddy hounds at a huntsman's beck and call.

*

When he heard my name
he came like a crow,
blessed and iridescent
in the rising sun,
giant striding the sea,
prince with his fleet of ships,
brother with a starling
cupped in his nesting hands.

BREAKING STONES

Out in the dusk
day after day
breaking stones,
summer and winter,
aching bones.

Nothing but dirt-tracks,
nothing but muddy ruts
for a horse and cart,
till they smashed stones
to smithereens.

Under the country lanes
where we dawdle in summer
picking blackberries,
swishing at nettles with sticks,
are their broken stones.

Under the tarmac of every road
every motorway,
lie the old tracks
and the stones they broke,
the stones they sold.

Winter and summer
stones for bread,
and bread for stones,
till their old bones ached
from breaking stones.

THE VILLAGE SHOP

Push the door. Ssh! Don't tell.
Listen for the old shop bell.
Imagine what they used to sell
fifty years ago –
Gobstoppers and Cherry-lips,
Humbugs, Sherbet, Lemon Pips
in little pointed paper slips.

Home from school, to the shop,
Beano, butter, lemon pop,
papers, stamps, ring-ring, non-stop.
And only yesterday –
Flip-flops, knickers, Pogs and wellies,
string and bottle gas and jelly,
sugar, carrots, vermicelli.

Now we drive to the supermarket.
Fumes and traffic. Stop and park it.
Fill the trolley. Pay by credit.
No more running down the street
when we run out of milk. No treats.
No kind hand with extra sweets.

No shop. No school. No bus. No train.
No quiet little country lanes.
just fumes and ozone in the air
and hurry, hurry everywhere.

THE HONEY MAN

The tin trunk rusts in a red pool
with its cargo of old frames,
crumbling honeycomb dark with pollens
and a dried glisten of wings
from dead summers.

By the gate, six feet from the car,
the abandoned hive the wild swarm
took over last year, that we meant
to move in winter as they slept
before the March sun woke them.

From the car we watch behind glass.
He comes through the dusk
in his space suit and veil,
calming the bees with the smoker
stuffed with smouldering cloth.

He lifts off the roof
and is jewelled with bees.
The air strums with a million stings
as they settle on the glass eye to eye
with the children.

At moonrise, before bed, we take turn
to press our ears against the hive,
to breathe in the honey, and listen
to a million cooling wings
beating like a city in a box.

STORM

The cat lies low, too scared
to cross the garden.

For two days we are bowed
by a whiplash of hurricane.

The hill's a wind-harp.
Our bones are flutes of ice.

The heart drums in its small room
and the river rattles its pebbles.

Thistlefields are comb-and-paper
whisperings of syllable and bone

till no word's left
but thud and rumble of

something with hooves or wheels,
something breathing too hard.

SUMMER-WATER SONNET

Summer-water's puddled, paddled, swum,
sailed, crossed, forded, squandered, spun,
worn like scales, jewellery, chain-mail,
to make a horse's mane, a mermaid tail,
to gather in armfuls, smash to smithereens,
to dig a channel for a little stream,
to drink from cupped hands on the mountain road,
to splash, to leap, to scream at, to off-load
in bucketfuls in a sand castle moat,
to float your poppy petals like silk boats,
to fish, to look in, see your own face blurred,
make mirrors for the moon, dragonflies, birds,
to get up in early dazzle and to be
first footprint on the shore, first in the sea.

THE HAND-GLASS

Look through the glass
at the palm of your hand
and bring to mind
what is too small to see:

a spiral of weightless stuff
like the house of a wasp,
but microscopically small, husk
no air is thin enough to thread.

And it turns out to be
the cast-off skin of a green fly,
that, being made of star-dust,
knows all about galaxies.

LETTERS FROM BOSNIA

Wales spelt *Vales*
on the brown envelope
from Vites to Llanidloes.
Inside a bundle of pages,
little illuminated manuscripts
of gilded Easter eggs,
scenes from a European spring
we'd all know anywhere,
an afternoon's work from the class in Vites.
'Dear Ben,' says one,
'You are my friend. Write me. Misha.'

Quietly, heads bent over the pages,
the children write the first draft of a poem.
Outside April is all indecision,
daffodils over, lawns blurred with speedwell,
the cherries torn by a sharp rain.
In the photograph, yesterday's Misha is smiling.
A class group grinning, pulling faces.
They wave, thumbs up to the future.
Behind them, in the rendered wall of the school
are the bullet holes.

IF I LIVED

If I lived in a terraced house, traffic
  would shake me.

If I lived in a castle keep, the wind
  would wake me.

If I lived in a bungalow, I'd sleep
  downstairs.

If I lived in a tower block, I'd fly high
  in the air.

If I lived in a boat, I'd float
  on slow green water.

If I lived in a caravan, I'd be
  the traveller's daughter.

WINTER RIDDLE

My car has grown
a woolly cover, yours a crown.

The door-mat's disappeared.
The hedge has grown a beard.

The bin's a cornet. Laurel leaves
are spoonfuls. Along the eaves

a row of glossy swords.
Starlings on the wires strumming chords.

Crocus strikes a match. Birds
print on the lawn their lines of words.

Trees wear fur. Wire has learned to knit.
Sheep aren't white. Grubby as a *clwt*

in need of bleach, they're at the gate,
waiting for hay and grumbling that we're late.

Touch-down and lift-off, look, a crow's
been making angels in the snow.

OLD CAT

Another winter dawn. I can't remember
how many mornings we've begun together,
me sipping tea, she lapping top-of-the-milk,
crunching munchies, licking her rusty silk.

Like an old woman with a shabby coat
she dabs an old stain with a bit of spit,
combs her knots out with a tongue-washed paw,
then sits half-dreaming at the Rayburn door.

Old cat! Her walk is heavy now, and slow,
her coat is rough. One winter day I know
there may be no one at the morning window,
only her paw-marks across fallen snow.

That morning, I'll switch on the kitchen light
and she won't leap to the sill out of the night,
her green eyes gleaming, silently mouthing 'O!
Let me in out of the wind and snow!'

But here she is again with a cry at the door.
I open it a crack to wind and sleet
and a handful of flakes. She delicately shakes each foot
and prints her daisy-chain across the floor.

Kettle and cat and stove will doze together,
adjusting old hearts to the icy weather.
All day the house will simmer with her purr
like a loaf rising, the lift and fall of fur.

A VERY COLD LAMB

With a book to finish and umpteen things to do,
here I am kneeling in straw, with a young ewe
fussing and mothering about me, drying the lambs
she slithered from her hot womb into the stream
where we found them, took them for frozen or drowned.
Working together, my hair-drier and her breath,
we warm two shivering lambs from the brink of death.
One is so cold it can't open its mouth to cry
for shaking, shaking hungry death by the throat,
that fox with a taste for soft tissue, that bird of doom
after each intricate beautiful brain, each eye.
We work for an hour, the drier humming, the ewe
licking their syrups with her passionate tongue,
calling the blood to their limbs, liver, lungs,
each womb as small as a nut. The two lambs strive.
They're warming to the idea of staying alive.

58

A POEM A DAY

Read a poem every day.
They're short and made of lovely words,
friendly, small as little birds.
They're really easy to remember.
So January to December,
read a poem every day.

Sing a poem every day
to keep the boredom bug away,
and when you go out to play,
drum it, dance it, make it rhyme,
learn it off to pass the time.
Try a new one every day.

When you're lying in your bed
and you can't sleep, in your head
sing a verse or two instead
of counting sheep. To help your slumber
January to December,
see how many you remember.

Notes on some of the Poems

'The Paddle-Steamers' – p. 24.

Glen Usk, *Ravenswood* and *The Cardiff Queen* were three of the paddle steamers which used to take people across the Bristol Channel between South Wales and Somerset and Devon.

'Horse of the Sea' – p. 28.

In legend, a great water horse called Elidir carried seven-and-a-half men through the sea from Scotland to Wales. Seven men rode on the horse's back and one clung to his tail. One of the riders became King of north Wales. In those days the people of Wales, north-west Britain and south Scotland, which was called the Old North, all spoke one language: Welsh.

'Branwen's Songs' – p. 46.

The story of Branwen is one of the old British myths of the Mabinogi. Branwen was the daughter of Llŷr, and her brother was a giant called Brân. Branwen married the King of Ireland. The Irish courtiers spread lies about Branwen, and when the king heard them he banished her from the court and sent her to work in the castle kitchens. She taught the starling to say her name, and sent it across the Irish Sea to her brother, Brân. He guessed she was unhappy, and he waded through the sea to rescue her, towing a fleet of ships behind him.

'Letters from Bosnia' – p. 54.

During the war in the part of the former Yugoslavia known as Bosnia Herzogovina, the children of Llanidloes Primary School in Powys exchanged letters and photographs with the children of Vites. They became pen-friends.